Kickstart Music

EARLY YEARS 3-5yrs

MUSIC ACTIVITIES MADE SIMPLE

ANICE PATERSON

DAVID WHEWAY

Contents

Introducing Kickstart

The Kickstart Music series is written specifically with the generalist primary teacher in mind. Kickstart Music 1, 2 and 3 cover the whole of Key Stage 1 and 2, and Kickstart Music Early Years is for under-fives. The authors firmly believe that every teacher can offer a positive musical experience to the children in his or her class.

Using Kickstart Music Early Years

The materials are divided into six sections: Listening, Rythm, Moving, Singing, Exploring and Creating. However, progression in music is not always linear and it is perfectly acceptable for them to be used in a different order. Where it is essential to have done certain other activities first it will say so in the text.

The section headings are fairly arbitrarily chosen. For example, rhythm activities will sometimes include poems, listening activities will sometimes include movement. The categories are more to do with a particular focus, but often set within a more holistic context.

The ideas here are designed to enable children to learn to listen, to make music, to feel and appreciate music and to respond to it in a variety of ways. They can be used inside and outside, at any time of day, for short or long periods. The activities have been tried and tested successfully in the classroom.

Most activities are not just a single lesson plan. Some may last for ten minutes and serve as warm-up activities for others. Some may be ideal to do in conjunction with other areas of the curriculum. Many activities will need revisiting and further practice to achieve success. Remember that in music repeated practice, doing things over and over again, is very important.

Local and national guidance dates quickly, so relating the activities too closely to current statutory documents has been avoided. There are certain experiences that music educationalists believe are important which have remained consistent over many years.

Music in an Early Years setting

Music within an early years context should at the very least offer:

- The opportunity for children to explore and to express themselves.
- The chance to enjoy sound in any context; to respond to/and create music through the use of their voices and bodies.
- Access to sound makers which should include appropriate percussion (tuned and untuned), but also the opportunity for exploring sound opportunities from materials such as paper, junk or recycled sources and the man-made/natural environment.
- The chance to develop an inner sense of pulse and rhythm through beat and rhythm activities and through rhyme.
- The opportunity to use sound to create music that is unique to themselves.

These materials offer support for the practitioner to grow in confidence, as well as opportunities for practitioners to support the musical development of the child. They are however equally useful to the more experienced and confident teacher/practitioner.

The materials cannot hope to encapsulate the individual and unique approaches that each adult and child will bring to their music experiences – and so we have attempted to avoid being too didactic – and hope that practitioners will adapt and shape these activities to suit their own experiences and environments.

Music with your class

Here are some very simple pointers showing how to get the best out of the music activities with your class.

Children copy adults

If you approach an activity in a positive, energetic and controlled way, the children will do the same.

Keep activities simple

Make sure that you know your materials well and aim to get the very best from each child. Don't try to do too much at any one time.

Children develop at different rates

In music, as in all other areas of the curriculum, keep an open mind about a child's musical potential. Children show it in a variety of ways.

Music is organised sound

Musical activity can happen anywhere – inside and outside. It can also happen with an infinite variety of sound sources – sounds in the environment, body sounds, sounds and rhythms from 'playing' junk as well as conventional instruments and voices.

Performance

Performance to an audience is rarely the intent of the activities here – although many of them may provide a short presentation of a few minutes, involving all the children, which parents/relations will appreciate. Develop opportunities to value stages of the process of music making.

Encourage children to care for instruments

If using instruments with a class, have them ready and close at hand at the start of the lesson to avoid losing time, and don't keep children waiting for too long before using them.

Children bring with them a wealth of musical experience

Young children bring with them musical experience from outside school, particularly from their families. Encourage them to be inventive, to sing to themselves, to try out new ideas. Their parents/ carers, relations and other members of the local community may also bring musical skills that can be shared with the class and the school.

Develop clear ways of controlling noise

Use definite signals for stopping and starting and expect quick responses. In some music activities expect lots of noise. Try to be tolerant of it. Music cannot exist without it. Encourage the tolerance of colleagues by explaining what you are doing and why.

Encourage children to care for Instruments.

If using instruments for a class, have them ready and close at hand at the start of the session to avoid losing time and don't keep children waiting for too long before using them.

Learning across the curriculum.

Music at this stage lends itself to being very well integrated into a child's total learning experience. Many activities in this book include the use of stories and rhymes and other aspects of language development, painting and pictures, scientific development, numbers and counting. Other obvious inter-relationships may involve skills of a personal or social nature such as developing physical coordination, discrimination, decision-making, self-confidence, self-discipline, participation, cooperation, tolerance and cultural awareness.

This section includes activities which develop children's ability to take turns and work with others, listen carefully to quiet sounds, rhythms and pitches, and differentiate between them, and listen and respond to music with concentration.

Be Still

1. Children sit as quiet and as still as possible. Listen to any sounds that are going on around for no more than half a minute.

2. Talk about what everyone heard. The list might include;
   - A car revving up.
   - Someone walking down the corridor outside.
   - Someone coughing.
   - The radiator humming.

3. Listen again for another half a minute. Some children may hear some new sounds now it's clear to them what is expected. Talk about it again and add to the list.

4. Talk about what they've heard. What makes the sound of the car? What is it actually making the sound when someone walks down the corridor? Which direction did the sounds come from?

5. Make up a map of what they've heard, reflecting the direction the sounds come from.

PURPOSE
To develop children's awareness of sounds.

EXTENSION

1. Play this whenever you are outside – in the playground, a walk through town, in different classrooms. Encourage them to do it at home and tell you about it next day.

Make a recording of sounds you hear in the market place/shopping mall when shopping. Play it back to the children to see if they can identify what they hear.

Play and respond

1. Tap the instrument, then hold it in front of the child and encourage her to play back. Encourage the concept of turn-taking between yourself and the child.

2. Pairs of children come out, one making a sound on the drum and the other copying it.

3. Play the simple rhythms of words and play what you say:
    - Beat the drum (beating the drum in time).
    - Shake the box (shaking the box in time).
    - Clap your hands.

   Children in turn copy the same rhythm, saying the same words.

4. Play a very simple rhythm (without words) for a child to copy. The child plays back the same rhythm. Keep it very simple – three or four beats only. Play to another child, and another.

5. If space allows, groups of children take it in turns to drum in time whilst the other children march or move around the room in time. Keep encouraging them to listen and keep in time. Many will not manage it and need plenty of practice to eventually get it right.

EXTENSION

Children can take turns and copy accurately rhythms they hear played.

PURPOSE
To develop careful listening and responding, as well as developing children's willingness to take turns.

RESOURCES
Drum, plus other sound makers.

Where is it?

1. One child leaves the room.

2. Everyone else spreads out all over the room.

3. One child has an instrument (eg, maracas) and plays it quietly behind his back. The other children pretend they have the maracas/instrument.

4. Child outside returns and listens carefully trying to locate where the very quiet sound is coming from.

5. They move amongst the children and put a hand on the shoulder of the child that they think has the maracas/instrument.

6. When the sound is found, repeat the activity with another child.

EXTENSION

Teacher or leader whispers the name of an animal into each child's ear – making sure there are two of each kind in the room. Children close their eyes and make their own animal noise while moving around the room. Can they find their 'partner' making the same noise? When they find partners they go to sit in 'Noah's Ark'

PURPOSE
To develop the ability to listen to and locate very quiet sounds or those that are difficult to distinguish.

RESOURCES
A variety of instruments that ring, or make an obvious sound eg, handbells, finger cymbals, small maracas.

REMEMBER
Sounds made must be very quiet indeed. Everyone has their hands behind their backs pretending to have the instruments.

Who's there?

1. Child A, eg, Suzi, closes her eyes and the teacher chooses Child B to say hello to them, 'Hello Suzi'.

2. Child A has to identify Child B by the tone of their voice.

3. Child B closes eyes and Child C says hello. And so on.

EXTENSION

1. Play 'I'm looking for a partner'. Choose a child to say the following rhyme. You might want to demonstrate it first.

   'I'm looking for a partner,
   To play my little game.
   Please say, "hello,"
   And I'll tell you your name'.

2. One child with eyes closed is led round circle of children, then tries to identify which child says "Hello."

3. Children try to disguise their voices by speaking in unusual ways, eg, high-pitch, low-pitch, whiny, posh, nasally.

4. Children sing their question, for instance, 'Can you guess who I am?' normally, or in unusual ways (high pitch, low pitch, whiny, posh, nasally).

PURPOSE
Identify another child by listening carefully to the timbre of their voice.

GLOSSARY

TImbre – quality of sound. The colour of a sound – the means of distinguishing between different qualities of sound.

For instance, how one is able to distinguish between the voices of two different singers singing the same song or between different instruments playing at the same time.

Who's next?

1. Give an instrument to one child, who plays the instrument while he walks round the circle looking for another child to hand it over to.

2. The chosen child takes the instrument, plays it, then gets up and walks around looking for the next child. And so on.

3. Give an instrument to another child as well. Repeat, encouraging the children with instruments to involve everyone in the group.

4. As children progress, add extra instruments until three or four are being played and passed around the circle.

5. Encourage children to listen to the 'music' that everyone is making while they're playing.

EXTENSION

A child with an instrument (or the teacher) plays a steady pulse on his instrument. The rest of the group think of a song they know, to sing along to the pulse,

Slow pulse:	'Hickory, Dickory, Dock'.
	'Incy Wincy Spider'.
	'Humpty Dumpty'.

Fast pulse:	'One man went to mow'.
	'Skip to my Lou'.
	'Pop goes the weasel'.

Melody lines and more information on resources can be found on p64 or at the Kickstart Music area of www.acblack.com/music.

PURPOSE
To encourage turn-taking and working with others.

RESOURCES

A variety of percussion instruments and sound makers.

Calm down music

1. Everyone lies on the floor if there is space, as still as they can.

2. Play some gentle music and let it wash over them, perhaps for up to about three minutes, depending on however long they can remain contentedly still. Don't talk while the music is on – let them just feel it.

3. Next time you hear the same music, or when the children begin to get a bit restless, encourage them to roll very slowly from side to side with the music. And the next time – gently move their arms in the air above them.

4. All the time be very quiet yourself and, as far as possible, don't intrude into their feeling the music. Let the music do the work.

5. When they are used to listening to music for a sustained length of time, do so sitting up – and encourage gentle stretching and bending movements or swaying from side to side.

Use music that you like yourself. It doesn't matter what style it is in. If you like it you will communicate your own good feelings about it. But make sure what you choose is fairly gentle and quiet to start with.

PURPOSE

To give children the opportunity to feel music played to them and to develop some concentration in doing so.

RESOURCES

Any recorded music which is not too loud or fast, eg, blues, slow movements of classical music. (Try ClassicFM radio, website) .

There are more resource suggestions on p64 and at the Kickstart Music section of www. acblack.com/music.

REMEMBER

This is an ideal activity for after lunch or just before home time. Hearing familiar music at specific times can enhance children's feelings of security.

Don't insist that they move as you suggest. The movements are a suggestion that will help them to listen for longer if they get restless. If they want to just listen and not move at all, let them.

Tell the children what the music is called, so they can ask for it again by name.

Statues

1. Decide on a sound to use as the signal to move and then freeze like a statue when the sound stops. The sound might be quite loud or very quiet – eg, whistling, humming, triangle trilling, drum rubbing.

2. The children move about the room to the sound (skipping, dancing, swirling, crawling) but freeze immediately when the sound ceases. Then again. And again.

3. Using a different sound as the signal, do the same movements. When the sound stops, children run to specific agreed points, such as hoops laid out on the floor, or to the four corners of the room. When it starts again they move back to the centre until it stops again.

EXTENSION

1. Play ascending notes on tuned percussion or a keyboard. Children listen hard and decide whether they will growing plants (sounds glissando (gliding) upwards) or plants dying off before winter (sounds glissando (gliding) downwards). Children grow like flowers with the sound. They revert to seed shapes, or become falling leaves when the notes descend.

2. Children move to a simple repeated tune on tuned percussion (eg a sequence of four notes repeated).
They listen for when the notes are played in a different sequence or at a different speed. When they hear the change, they freeze.

A possible repeated sequence with last sequence reversed:

CDEF CDEF CDEF CDEF CDEF CDEF CDEF FEDC

A possible repeated sequence with last sequence at half speed:

CDEF CDEF CDEF CDEF CDEF CDEF CDEF C – D – E - F

PURPOSE
To develop attentive listening.

RESOURCES
A few small instruments.

Tuned percussion/ keyboard for the Extension activity.

Surround sound

1. The following activity could be done in the classroom, another part of the school, or whilst on a visit (eg, a farm, the countryside, near the building site, in the town, at the seaside).

2. Ask the children to sit or lie on the floor with their eyes closed, and to remain still for 20 seconds.

3. Talk about the sounds that were heard during the silence.
   - Can they remember what sounds they heard?
   - Do they imagine they heard some sounds?
   - Can they identify any of the sounds?
   - What were the sounds like (loud, harsh, smooth, gentle, tapping whirring)?

3. Can the children find ways to imitate some of the sounds either vocally or on instruments?

4. The children might go on to create sounds which they put together to re-create the original scene back in the classroom.

EXTENSION

Collect things on a visit (leaves, sticks, paper, photos) and make a large 'Memory Collage' of them, along with children's drawings of the visit.

Each child thinks about sounds for the objects in the collage and finds sounds with or without sound makers. Agree who plays their sounds and in what order. Everyone then plays/ sings/performs their sounds in front of the collage picture as a performance – maybe inviting someone else in to listen. Do 'Be still' on p5 first.

PURPOSE
To identify sounds and develop a musical vocabulary.

RESOURCES

A variety of percussion and sound makers for Extension.

Materials to make collage.

REMEMBER

It is harder to do this with quiet sounds because it requires greater concentration. It is good to play very quietly sometimes as this develops listening and attention skills.

High and low

1. Look at the xylophone (vertically) with the children and talk about your fingers walking up and down it.

2. Then play up and down the xylophone with a beater and see if they can recognise the sound going up and down as well.

3. Play two notes, one low and one high.

4. Children stand for the high notes and sit for the low.

5. Now play up and down the xylophone again. The children gradually rise up out of their seats as high as they can while you play up the instrument. Then when you play down, they slowly move to sit down again.

EXTENSION

1. All children have access to an instrument. Everyone decides which instruments play high or low sounds or both. This time the teacher stretches high and the children play the high sound. The teacher crouches low and the children with low instruments play – and so on.

2. Use little yellow stickers and a large piece of paper or board. A child plays a note. Two other children take a yellow sticker and put it as high or as low as they think it is on the paper/board. You will end up with a mass of yellow stickers in order of how they were played. If the children understand it well enough you could 'play' the 'score' again from the stickers.

3. Play the high and low notes on the piano for the same activity. There is a huge range from top to bottom so they are fairly recognisable – but the link between physical 'high' notes and the 'top' of the instrument is not so obvious.
Play in conjunction with 'Up and down' on p38.

PURPOSE
To respond to sound with body movement and encourage the identification of high and low sounds.

RESOURCES

A xylophone or glockenspiel stood on end with high (smaller) notes at the top. This allows the children to make a physical association between high and low (see illustration below).

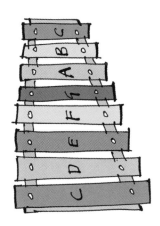

Hand signs

1. Ask the children to watch the puppet carefully. They will pick up their instruments, but only play when the puppet moves. When it is still they should be quiet.

2. At first try stopping and starting. When they have the idea, try making very small movements with the puppet. Do the children follow by playing quietly? If not, remind them to watch the puppet carefully.

3. Now try a range of movements to get a range of sounds, from loud to very quiet and silent. The puppet makes big movements, the children play loudly, small movements, softly.

4. When the children are confident, invent some simple hand signs to replace the puppet:

   Hands apart – play. Hands together –silent.

5. As with the puppet, introduce a range of hand signs to encourage a range of dynamics.

6. Choose a song to sing that the children know well. Sing the song asking the children to watch your hand signs for louds and softs. Can they change the dynamics as you alter the hand signs? This requires patience and practice.

PURPOSE
To develop attentiveness and control when playing.

RESOURCES
Puppet.

Variety of instruments or soundmakers.

GLOSSARY

Dynamics – the different volumes or levels at which sounds are played, eg, loud, soft, getting louder getting softer.

This section includes activities which encourage children to develop a strong sense of pulse, the ability to feel and move to rhythms in time and to understand the use of repetitions to make music. Many will also help to develop their co-ordination and control of their bodies to help them play instruments.

Clap your hands

1. Clap your hands to the tune of 'Baa baa black sheep' first to get the children used to clapping in time.

   X   x   x   x
   Clap your hands and tap your knees
   X   x   x   x
   Clap again now if you please
   X   x   x   x
   Tap your shoulders left and right
   X   x   x   x
   Fold your arms and all sit tight

2. Sing the above song through with the children. Make up your own tune or chant the lyrics. When they know it well, add the clapping. They will not all be able to do both at once.

3. Show the children extra actions and invite them to join in. For example, on the words 'Fold your arms' – fold your arms in the air then bring them down on the beat.

4. Go very slowly and check that all the children have made the actions. When they have all mastered them you can make it harder by going faster.

5. Add variety by using different actions, for example:
   - Fold your arms and whistle ('wshhhh').
   - Turn around and touch your toes.

PURPOSE
To develop a sense of beat through actions songs.

Tap it, clap it

1. Start by tapping a simple rhythm on your knees, for example, to any of the phrases:
   'Two huge feet'
   'Hairy scary frogs'
   'Bangers and mash'
   'Beans and custard'
   'Milk and sandwiches'

2. Ask the children to join in and copy the rhythm.

3. Now select one of the rhythms to tap repeatedly. Ask the children to join in keeping it steady. When they can all do this, try a new rhythm.

4. Now clap or tap various parts of your body (head, shoulders, hips) for simple rhythms which the children copy, for example:

   'Beans and custard'
   (clap   clap tap tap)

5. Select a different sequence which the children copy, for example:

   'Two huge feet'
   (tap tap   clap)

6. Try two groups playing different sequences together. Can they play at the same time and keep it going?

EXTENSION

1. When the children can keep one of the rhythms going reliably, try singing a song to go with it so they become the regular rhythmic backing, or ostinato (see Glossary box). They may need to keep saying the phrase while they do so to keep them in time.

2. Some children could 'play' the rhythm on the table while everyone else sings the song. Can they keep it going?

PURPOSE
To copy simple rhythms.

REMEMBER

This is a short activity to get children in the mood for doing other rhythmic work. Use it frequently and follow it with another activity.

GLOSSARY

Ostinato – A rhythm or tune which repeats itself continuously, in a way that can be used as an accompaniment to part of, or throughout, a piece of music.

Do as I do

1. Children sit where they can see. They watch carefully, copy your actions and change their action when you do. In the first instance these actions can be non-rhythmic, such as washing hands, yawning and stretching, waving and smiling, crouching and growling, shaking cobwebs out of legs and arms.

2. Now set up a steady tap on your knees. The children copy.

3. Change the rhythm. The children listen hard and change too. And then change again.

4. Try repeating rhythms like these:
   'Salt and pepper, salt and pepper.'
   'Soooooooup slurpy, sooooooup slurpy.'
   'Pop goes fzzzzzzzz! Pop goes fzzzzzzzzzz!'

5. When all the children have joined in, change the actions to – tapping head/shoulders/arm. Wait until all the children are copying before changing again. The children change quickly to your actions.

6. When the children can maintain a steady beat through any of the actions and rhythms you choose, find some recorded music and play along with it.

7. Listen to a snatch of the music and practise steps 2 and 4 of this activity again, playing a steady tap or word rhythm with the music and the children copy.

8. Keep trying new rhythms and word patterns to the music while the children copy. When you find a particularly good one, keep it going together for longer. This might even develop into a mini dance movement.

PURPOSE
To develop a sense of pulse.

RESOURCES

Music with a strong beat for the extension; for example, any dance music or big band music.

REMEMBER

The most important thing is to help the children to maintain a steady beat, even if they make mistakes in the actions or words. Moving rhythmically can help a lot.

Here we come to play

SONG

'Here we come to play' to the tune of 'One man went to mow' (below):

Here we come to play,
Here we come together.
Number one is (name of child, eg, Anisha Desai),
When we play together.

1. Children in a large circle – instruments in the middle.

2. Organise the children into a circle and decide who will be 'number one today' (see line three). Number one collects an instrument from the centre as the song is sung – and returns to his/her place.

3. As you reach the child's name in the song, the teacher, or everyone sings the child's name.

4. Repeat the song and number one child plays while you all sing. Select the number two child (eg, by touching a child on the shoulder).

5. Number two child plays along with the next repeat of the song. You may wish to give them a chance to play solo as well at the end of the song.

6. Repeat with new children each time you repeat the song.

EXTENSION

1. Sing about child one, the child two, building up each time a child is added.

2. Try counting backwards at the end of line 3, (as in 'One man went to mow' eg, 'Number two is Rosie Briggs, Number one is Ishmal Patel, when we play together').

PURPOSE
Simple greeting/ counting song which names the children, builds a texture and encourages children to take turns.
Also – a calm way of distributing instruments.

RESOURCES
Enough percussion for each child to have an item.

REMEMBER
Encourage every child to play to the beat of the song. You could allow all the children to play along as you accumulate players but don't add more than five players or it will sound too muddled.

The talking drum

RHYME

The children try stepping on the spot to the beat. Begin, left, right… before starting the rhyme

'Pass the beater to the beat
Pass the beater, move your feet
Pass the beater, don't hold on
Pass the beater, you're the one!'

PURPOSE
To develop children's co-ordination and sense of rhythm.

RESOURCES

A drum and a large beater.

1. Play the game 'Pass the beater' using the rhyme above. Pass a beater round the circle like in the game 'Pass the parcel'.

2. When the rhyme stops (on the word, 'One!'), the child with the beater comes forward and taps a short rhythm on a drum.

3. It may help to give the child some phrases to choose from, such as:

'Beat the | Drum'.
 X   x | **X**

'I | like to play the | tambourine'
 x | **X**   x **X**   x | **X** x **X**

4. The other children can clap the child's rhythm back to him/her.

5. 'Pass the beater' rhyme starts again round the circle.

EXTENSION

This works well passing the beater in time to some recorded music but make sure that the beat is fairly secure first.
For more information on songs and resources go to p64 or visit the Kickstart Music section of www.acblack.com/music.

Wiggly worm

1. With the children begin a repeat count from 1 to 4, putting more emphasis on number 1.

   1 2 3 4, 1 2 3 4, **1** 2 3 4, **1** 2 3 4

2. Wait until all the children are saying the numbers to a steady beat.

3. Now tell the children you will repeat the count, but this time they will all wriggle on number (beat) 3. Practise wriggling.

4. Repeat the activity until everyone is remembering to wriggle most of the time on number (beat) 3.

5. Repeat the game with different actions (jump, crouch, stretch) on different numbers.

6. Change the count to 1-6, or 1-8.

EXTENSION

1. Children each have an instrument or sound maker. They decide on a number on which they will make their sound. Practise with all the number ones playing on number one. Repeat for the other numbers.

2. Now begin a steady count, encouraging each child to play their sound, but only on their number. Try and listen to the resulting music.

PURPOSE
To begin to be aware of beats in a bar and to feel a regular pulse.

REMEMBER

This activity helps children to feel the regular pulse that most music is based on. If you are playing some simple dance music with an obvious number of beats you could do the same activity.

Bricks and mortar

RHYME

Bricks and mortar (children echo the leader),

'(Leader):   Mix the mortar slip, slop, slap!
(Children): Mix the mortar slip, slop, slap!
(Leader):   Hear the bricks go tip, top, tap!
(Children): Hear the bricks go tip, top, tap!'

1. Everybody in a circle, kneeling. Talk about builders and what they do.

2. Learn the rhyme, encouraging the children to echo each line.

3. Whilst saying, 'Mix the mortar slip, slop, slap,' gently stroke the ground rhythmically with inward movements, alternating left and right hands. Encourage the children to copy your movements.

4. Whilst saying, 'Hear the bricks go tip, top, tap,' alternate one fist above the other (as in the rhyme 'One potato') as if building a wall. Again, encourage the children to copy the action rhythmically.

5. Divide the children into two groups. Once the children can do the actions fairly rhythmically, try with the 'mortar' group with shakers and bricks with tappers. The shaker group shake their rhythm and the tappers add theirs.

6. Encourage the children playing instruments to shake or tap to the beat if possible.

PURPOSE
To say and play simple rhythms.

RESOURCES

Shakers - maracas, cartons or crisp tubes filled with dried peas or sugar.

Tappers – claves, woodblocks, tulip blocks, cut up broom handles.

REMEMBER

Keep a steady pulse. Repeating small sections of rhymes and tunes will ensure effective results.

Oak and acorn

1. Introduce the children to the picture cards (below). Show them how the oak changes into an acorn when the cards are flipped over.

2. Lay the four cards down, all with the oak sides showing. To a steady beat, say:

   'Oak   Oak   Oak   Oak'

3. The children join in as you repeat the phrase. Then ask the children to clap the words as you say them (clapping on each word, 'oak'). Some children will find this quite difficult.

4. Now flip one of the cards over and say the new phrase. For example:

   'Oak   Acorn   Oak   Oak'

5. Children join in as you repeat the phrase. Try clapping the new phrase. Remember that you will clap twice for 'Acorn' as it has two syllables. Can the children suggest new rhythm phrases, by turning over different cards?

EXTENSION

1. Children can try tapping the rhythms on a tambour or drum.

2. Try singing a made-up tune to the children with the rhythm as you turn the cards over.

3. Try using blank cards sometimes so the children have to think of a rest between the other cards. Keep up the regular four time even with the rest.

PURPOSE
To play simple rhythms.

RESOURCES

Oak and Acorn cards The cards have a picture of an oak one side, and an acorn on the flip side. Photocopy and enlarge the illustrations on this page to create cards. These images can also be found at the Kickstart Music area of www.acblack.com/music.

REMEMBER

This activity helps children to feel the regular pulse that most music is based on. If you are playing some simple dance music with an obvious number of beats you could do the same activity.

Chuffa train

RHYME

Chuffa train

'Chuff, chuff, chuffa train,
Clicketty, clacketty, wind or rain,
Over the bridge and under the lane,
Down to the sea and back again.'

1. Learn the rhyme until everyone knows it well.

2. Say it over and over again in different ways. For example:
   - Start with the train in the distance, with each repeat get closer (louder) and then with the last repeat go off again into the distance (quieter).

   - Get gradually quicker as the train leaves the station, say the rhyme fast as it is travelling, and say it again with a big slow down to a stop as it arrives at its destination.

3. Make a train: A line of some of the children moves around the room as a train, stepping rhythmically as they keep repeating the words, 'Chuffa train, chuffa train', as an ostinato (see Glossary box). Whilst that group moves, another group says the full rhyme as many times as necessary for the train to cover the ground.

4. The next time you do it, different children take the part of the train.

EXTENSION

Find some vocal sounds/movements for the seaside (seagulls, rolling shingle, waves). Incorporate the sounds during/at the end of the train's journey.

PURPOSE

To move
and chant rhythmically.

GLOSSARY

Ostinato – A rhythm or tune which repeats itself continuously, in a way that can be used as an accompaniment to part of, or throughout, a piece of music.

Animal grids

1. The children are assisted to create short rhythmic phrases using pictures of, for example, farmyard animals. By choosing words of one and two syllables, simple but varied rhythms can be established, for example:

'Cow	Cow	Chi – cken	Cow.'
'Pig – let	Cow	Cow	Pig-let.'
'Duck-lings	Cow	Pig-let	Duck-lings'.

2. Once the children can say these phrases, they move on to clapping them and/or playing them on instruments.

    Note: children of this age will often say the phrases, whilst not necessarily clapping/playing every syllable. It is useful to support them, for instance by clapping along with them.

3. Split the children into groups of animals (for example a cow group, a piglet group). Say, clap and/or play different phrases as pictures of their animals are held up.

4. Practise saying, then clapping, then playing each of the rhythms until secure.

5. Divide the group into two – each smaller group with a responsibility for maintaining one of the short rhythmic phrases, for example:

'Cow	Cow	Chi – cken	Cow.'
'Duck-lings	Cow	Pig-let	Duck-lings.'

EXTENSION

Try building to more than two groups. Each group will ideally be led by an adult – as this is quite a challenge.

PURPOSE

To say, clap, play simple rhythms.

RESOURCES

Pictures of animals, which may be drawings on paper plates.

REMEMBER

It is useful if an assistant can help lead the groups. As you divide into more groups it becomes more important for them to have an adult per group.

Moving

This section includes activities which will help children develop the ability to move freely and rhythmically to music, develop their co-ordination for the playing of instruments and have the opportunity to respond to the music they hear with feeling.

Peter and the wolf

1. Listen to the extracts of music, and talk to the children about how the composer has tried to recreate the character of the people/animals in the story.

2. The children find appropriate movements for the characters in the story. In the case of 'Peter and the Wolf' these would be:

   Grandad – walking as if with a stick and holding his back
   Wolf – padding, prowling, rearing head and looking around furtively.
   Bird – fast movements, flying and flapping around.
   Duck – sad and mournful, swimming slowly in the pond.
   Peter – dancing and jumping – walking along arms outstretched as if balancing.

3. Play the music again, asking the children to make their movements to the music. Try playing short extracts with contrasting characters, so that children can switch from one type of movement to the another. This activity does not have to be done with the story of 'Peter and the wolf' but any extract of music referring to strong characters.

PURPOSE
To be aware of the characteristics and moods found in music.

RESOURCES

Extracts of music referring to strong characters, such as 'Peter and the Wolf' (Prokofiev).

Visit p64 or the Kickstart Music area of www.acblack. com/music for more information on resources.

Sleepy bones

1. Pass an instrument silently around the circle. Start with one that is easy to keep quiet such as a wooden block. A more difficult one needing much greater control is a tambourine.

2. Next, children should try to pass the instrument without 'waking' a puppet or fluffy toy held by the teacher. If there is a sound, the puppet looks up in the direction that the sound came from. (It is best not to do this too dramatically in order that the children don't lose the stillness and seriousness of the exercise).

3. Now a child sits in the middle of the circle, pretending to be asleep. The children should try and pass the instrument without 'waking' the child.

4. How many times did he/she wake up? How many times do they hear the instrument as it is passed round?

5. Can the child in the middle with her eyes closed point to where the sound was coming from?

PURPOSE
To control sounds, develop concentration and value stillness.

RESOURCES
Fluffy toy or puppet.
A variety of instruments.

REMEMBER
This activity can be played as a warm-up for just a few minutes before doing something livelier. But it can be turned to often within any session to calm children down. It could be used later when handing out instruments as part of teaching the children control when using them.

The frightened tortoise

1. Children find a space.

2. Talk with the children about tortoises and what they do when they are frightened. Perhaps look at a short video of a tortoise from the internet.

3. Bang the drum loudly – all the children curl up and hide their heads 'in their shells.'

4. Begin playing the drum very quietly. As it continues very quietly the 'tortoises' become more confident and gradually extend their limbs from their shells, feeling the space around them, and moving around.

5. Now play some music. As above, play it quite softly to start with and gradually turn up the volume for the children to emerge and move. When the music stops, tortoises pop back inside their shells. This encourages movement and careful listening.

6. Use the same technique on the music player to encourage the children to be:
    *   Hedgehogs uncurling – then suddenly curling up again.
    *   Birds soaring and landing.
    *   A cat stalking then pouncing on an insect/ball of string.
    *   A rabbit hopping around then disappearing down its burrow.
    *   The child asleep and waking up very slowly, then jumping out of bed.

PURPOSE
To provide an opportunity to combine sound, movement and feeling.

RESOURCES

A drum.

A choice of music on a music player. Any music will work – choose something you like yourself and you will communicate good feelings about it.

Let's dance

1. Everyone finds a space.

2. Play one extract of music and children move around the room stepping in time to the music. Concentrate on helping them find the beat to step on. They won't necessarily all manage it.

3. Think of new movements to use. Children move to the music with simple stepping, swaying or waving movements. For instance:
   - Two children hold a ribbon and sway, or all children have a ribbon.
   - Children sit facing pairs with feet touching. They hold hands and sway back and forth.
   - Children stand face to face in two long lines while pairs of children take turns to dance down the centre.

4. Now use two extracts of music with contrasting beats/moods. Give them a short listen and time to think about moves to each of them. Now play each piece in full, one after the other and the children move their different ways. They might do the following:
   - Samba – bounce up and down, in time.
   - Waltz – sway lazily from side to side, in time.
   - Irish Jig – jump or run about the room as fast as the music suggests.

5. Ask them to show others some of their favourite movements, with the music on again.

6. Discuss the differences. The moods of the music; the different moves they all made. Can the children describe how their movements were different for each contrasting piece – slower, more gentle, jumping.

PURPOSE
To begin to move in contrasting ways to contrasting pieces of music.

RESOURCES
Music for dancing with contrasting moods such as samba, reggae, African, pop, waltzes or music from well-known children's films.

REMEMBER
The extracts might be edited on an audio-recording program such as 'Audacity' so that one extract fades into another. There is more information on Music technology in the Kickstart Music are of www.acblack.com.

Ready now

SONG

To the tune of 'Boys and girls come out to play':

All hold hands – then we've begun,
Make a circle – and we'll have fun.
As we sing, we'll move in time,
*Ella, please will you tell us how.
*The selected child is then encouraged to share
an action, eg, waving arms.

1. Sing the song through while the children skip round in a circle.

2. Sing the song again and encourage individual children to offer an action when they are confident (line four features the chosen child's name).

3. Choose a child and agree what action they will share with the rest of the children. Now change the third line of each verse when the child gives you their action. For example:

'As we sing, we'll wave our arms.'
'As we sing, we'll jump up high.'

4. Repeat the song. Those who are confident enough sing the song along with the teacher. Everyone does the actions suggested and shown by the first child.

5. Other children are then chosen in turn to suggest another action. You may need to adapt the words slightly to fit the tune.

Other suggested actions: Walk in a ring, shake our hands, nod our heads, bounce about, touch our toes, pounce like lions, stretch up high, hop about.

PURPOSE
To join in singing together and suggest actions for songs.

RESOURCES
Tambour or other small drum.

REMEMBER
If singing for the first time, you might like to have a selection of suggestions before beginning. Later on don't worry if some children choose actions that have already been chosen.

Just like clockwork

1. The story of 'Coppélia' provides an interesting starting point for this activity, as much of the story takes place in a toy-maker's shop where the toys come to life. This activity works just as successfully if you do not use this story. You can talk about toys coming alive at night or watch 'Bagpuss' footage online.

2. Imagine a toy shop at night where the toys get up and dance. How would they dance? What movements would the toys make? Talk about the childrens' own toys. Do they dance whilst the children are asleep, and if so, how do they dance?

3. The children move like clockwork toys to the music, moving their hands, elbows, shoulders, arms, head, knees, legs and feet like machines.

4. Gradually each part goes limp - for instance, on the tap of a tambour, or as the music slows:
    *   An arm goes limp and hangs by the side.
    *   Then the other arm does the same.
    *   One leg goes wobbly- then the other.
    *   Head goes floppy.

5. Eventually the children stand like floppy scarecrows, swaying gently in the breeze.

6. Try the same activity with the children representing floppy dolls or string puppets.

7. Ask the children to bring in a toy of their own the next day to do the activity again.

PURPOSE
To respond to music through movement.

RESOURCES

Extract: 'Musique des automates from Coppélia' by Delibes

'What do you see?' from the film 'Chitty Chitty Bang Bang.' or any strongly rhythmical music.

Animal fair

1. Ask the children to name animals they might see if they went to Africa, India, the Antarctic or Australia.

2. What sounds do the animals make? Can the children imitate the sounds vocally? Once they have an idea of the sounds, explore percussion instruments or other sound makers to find sounds that can supplement the vocal sounds.

3. Ask the children to imitate the movements of the animals.

4. Perhaps they can find simple melodies (eg, two-note tunes) on tuned percussion to represent the animals. Discuss together whether these two-note tunes should be high or low (eg, high for small birds, low for elephants, low to high for kangaroos)?

5. Some of the children make their animal movements while others accompany with their vocal/instrumental sounds. The sounds could be structures to create simple sequences of sound and movement.

EXTENSION

Play some extracts from 'Carnival of the Animals' by Saint-Saëns – particularly the 'Elephant', and the 'Aviary' for children to move to.

PURPOSE
To imitate animal sounds and create movement in response to these sounds.

RESOURCES

Pictures of animals which have obvious sounds, such as elephants, lions, snakes, monkeys, penguins. Each picture is either on a stick to hold up, or pinned high up around the wall in different corners as a focus for each animal.

Extracts from 'Carnival of the Animals' by Saint-Saëns for the Extension activity.

Some tuned instruments and other sound makers.

Let's move

1. Play the first extract (no obvious beat) to the children and ask them to listen carefully and move to the music. It will probably help them if you join in. This might be moving around the room, or sitting and just moving their arms. The movements are likely to be quite small or gentle ones.

2. Then play the second extract (with the strong beat) to the children, and again ask them to move to the music.

3. When the children have moved to both extracts, ask them if they noticed the pieces were different from each other. It may help to ask them questions, such as:
   • Which piece of music made you want to dance more?
   • Which piece of music was peaceful?
   • Which was the loudest/quietest piece of music?
   • Did anyone recognise any of the instruments that were playing?

4. Create a short sequence of the pieces of music – eg, Piece A, then B, then A again. Children move appropriately to this ABA sequence.

PURPOSE
To move in different ways to music.

RESOURCES
Two extracts of music, one without an obvious beat. For example, try the start of a raga or the 'Adagietto' from Mahler's 5th symphony, and one with a strong beat, for instance Latin American music, pop music, waltz music, or a first movement of any Mozart Symphony.

Aquarium

1. Play an extract of music which sounds like water to the children (eg, 'Aquarium' or 'La Mer') and talk about the various ways creatures of the sea move such as:

   - Large fish – gliding and weaving.
   - Small fish – fluttering fins.
   - Jelly fish – pumping and gliding.
   - Sea horses – bobbing and rocking.
   - Scallops – snapping and darting.

2. Encourage the children to find ways of moving such as:

   - Running and changing direction.
   - Small fluttering finger movements using their arms to suggest movement.
   - Pumping arms by their sides and gliding.
   - Standing tall and bobbing forward.
   - Making large clapping movements and darting short distances.

3. Select one of the movements to move to while the music plays. Then change to another type of movement. The children wave ribbons and other materials to accentuate the movements.

4. Divide the groups into two or more types of sea creature to move to the music.

PURPOSE

To move sympathetically to music.

RESOURCES

'Aquarium' from 'Carnival of the Animals' by Saint Saëns. Or any other pieces of music which sound like water.

Coloured ribbons and pieces of material to wave.

REMEMBER

This could develop out of a trip to the seaside or a project on the sea. To perform the children's movements in front of a large sea collage would be perfect.

Expressive sound

1. Children sit in a circle.

2. Each child has an instrument or sound maker.

3. The conductor stands in the middle of the circle. Initially this might be an adult, but children should quickly be encouraged to take the lead.

4. Offer simple instructions to follow, for example:
   Hands by side = don't play. Hands in the air = play.

   Practise several times, with the children playing any sound on their instrument. It can take some time to follow and control being silent at exactly the right moment.

5. Begin to introduce new instructions, for example:
   Arms raised slowly = getting louder.
   Lowered slowly = getting quieter.

   Arms waved faster – sounds speed up, and so on.

   Encourage the children who are playing to follow the movements closely.

6. Encourage the conducting child to begin moving expressively to influence the ways sounds are made. They might make:
   • Smooth slow gliding movements.
   • Short snappy movements.
   • Rhythmic stepping/trotting.
   • Staying very still.
   • Growing bigger/smaller, and so on.
   How many ways can the moving child influence the way the sounds are played?

EXTENSION

Sing a song they know well and use your hands to indicate when you want them to sing softly or loudly.

PURPOSE

To encourage children to control stopping and starting sound and make decisions about sound quality.

RESOURCES

Music player.
Descriptive music.

More information on resources can be found at the Kickstart Music area of www. acblack.com/music.

REMEMBER

This activity can be done over many sessions in sections. It is very good for encouraging shy children to become involved in activities.

Singing

This section includes activities which will help children to find their voice, sing with enjoyment and improve their understanding of pitch. Many activities work well with small groups – especially where solo responses are to be encouraged.

Warm up your voice

Try some or all of the following activities to warm up the voice and help the children find their voices. Make sure they are standing, or sitting in a chair, rather than sitting on the floor, so they can breathe better. This helps the quality of the sound they make.

PURPOSE
To help children to develop ways of singing well.

1. **Articulation**
   - Make 'sh, sh, sh' train noises.
   - Make 'cluck cluck cluck' hen noises.
   - Sing or say lots of consonant words, well articulated and repeated lots of times – 'pop, dad, gig, tot, bob, sis, shush, viv'.
   - Sing tongue twisters on one note. Try these short, alliterative ones:
     Dancing dinosaurs.
     Loopy lunar landings.
     Laughing llamas.

REMEMBER

Not all children will physically be able to sing in tune at this stage – do not stop them trying. Singing entirely unaccompanied helps them to hear more accurately what they are singing than if percussion or piano is playing.

2. **Breathing**
   - Make siren noises – up as high as possible and down again.
   - Make 'ha, ha, ha', laughing noises.
   - Say or sing 'OOOOOOOOOOOO' for as long as you can (This can be difficult for some).

3. **Vocal cords**
   - Hum on one note – for as long as you can.
   - Say or sing 'OOOOOOOOOOOO' as if climbing up the (pitch) stairs – ie getting gradually higher.
   - Say or sing 'AAAAAAAAAAAA' as if coming down the stairs.

Singing well-known songs

1. Try singing songs which are well-known to the class and/ or to you in different ways:
   - Very softly. Can the children sing softly whilst still articulating the words?
   - Very slowly. You may need to find a way to maintain the beat – and not allow the song to become gradually faster.
   - Very cheerfully. Avoid singing loudly or they might shout.
   - With eyes closed. This can help children focus on the sound they are making.
   - To 'la/oo/ah/ee/pa'. This helps develop open vowel sounds. Try pretend stretching and yawning before singing.

2. Alternate lines by two groups of children so they can listen to each other:
   - Happily.
   - Sadly.
   - Crossly.
   - With actions.

3. Make an audio recording of the children and encourage them to talk about their performance. See if they comment on aspects of the performance, such as:
   - Were they too loud?
   - Did they get the words right?
   - Can you remember the last line? Let's sing it again.

PURPOSE
To explore the timbre of the voice.

GLOSSARY

Timbre – The colour or quality of the sound. The same note played on a trumpet and a guitar will have a completely different tone colour or timbre. Often described in terms like warm, dark, silky, harsh, smooth, brassy, mellow.

What's the news?

1. **Sing the register.** Instead of talking through the register – or just marking it off, make an event of it. Take two chime bar notes such as G and E which sounds like a cuckoo call. Sing like this and expect a sung answer from the children too .

   > (Teacher:) 'Is Sean here today?'
   > (Child:) 'Yes, I'm here today.'
   > (Everyone:) 'Yes, Sean's here today.' (Or perhaps 'Good morning Sean')

   Change the notes you use from time to time and the children copy whatever you sing. Make sure you pitch your voice high enough for them.

2. **Sing questions**. Once comfortable with the idea of the 'cuckoo' interval, try it at a slightly higher pitch. Tip: Using a xylophone to find a start note can be helpful.

3. **Share news** using the cuckoo interval (G and E).

   > (Teacher:) 'Who has news today? Gemma – tell us your news.'
   > (Child) – 'I've got a new sister.

   > Other ideas:
   > (Teacher:) 'Freya – what's your favourite food?'
   > (Child:) 'I like fish and chips. (with eating actions).

   > (Teacher:) Sanjay - 'what are you painting?'
   > (Child:) 'I'm painting a house' (with actions).

   > (Teacher:) 'Who's got a pet cat?'
   > (Children:) 'I've got a pet cat.'
   > (Everyone:) 'Stroke, stroke our pet cat' (with a stroking action).

PURPOSE

To develop children's singing voice through simple greetings/ action songs and give children a reason to sing solo.

RESOURCES

Chime bars G and E

REMEMBER

Use your skills as a teacher, and knowledge of your children to identify children with their news, and encourage participation with those children who might be reticent to contribute. Reticent children may only indicate with a monosyllabic response or maybe only a gesture – but this is a start that can be built on.

Up and down

1. Play any two notes, one low and one high. It is helpful to stand a xylophone or glockenspiel on its end, with the higher (smaller) bars at the top, so that children can make a visual association between high and low (see illustration below).

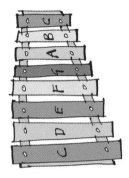

2. Children stand. For the high notes they raise their arms high up, stretching to the ceiling. For the low notes, they drop their arms down to the floor.

3. Ask children to lead selecting high/low notes to which others respond.

4. Now introduce a middle note. Children adopt a mid-way position.

5. For some children, maybe in a group, it may be possible to respond to four or five notes. For example:
   Low note = crouch.
   Low/middle note = squat.
   Middle = bend forward.
   Middle high = stand up.
   High note = stretch tall.

6. As the children get better at it, play notes closer together and expect them to move up and down in smaller stages.

EXTENSION

Try with another instrument, one you/another member of staff plays or a visiting instrumentalist/parent. The 'new' instrument may be harder because children won't be able to see whether the note is high or low.

PURPOSE

To identify high and low sounds (important to understand when singing) and respond to the pitch with body movement.

RESOURCES

A xylophone or glockenspiel stood on end with high (smaller) bars at the top – so children can make a physical and visual association between high and low. Make sure it's visible to all the children.

REMEMBER

As the interval decreases, discrimination becomes increasingly difficult – so don't expect children to respond so quickly.

Hills and dales

1. Ask children to respond to your movement of the puppet with their voices. A sudden rise from the floor to up high – whoosh. As if coming down a slide – 'wheeee'. As if in a car going up a steep hill slowly – 'mmmmmmmmmm'.

2. Tell the children that the puppet is going to go for a walk over the hills. Move the puppet as if it is walking up and down the hills.

3. Now ask the children to hum or 'la' while they watch the puppet. As the puppet goes higher, the children hum higher. They hum lower as the puppet goes down. (The children may well hum louder as they go higher). If the children are having difficulty, repeat step one above.

4. Ask a child to take the puppet for a walk. The other children respond with sounds to the puppet's movements. Encourage the child to move slowly enough for the others to respond.

5. Next, try vowel sounds, such as sustained 'ah' as you stretch up, 'oo' as you crouch down.

6. Ask the children to think of and imitate other sounds which get higher and lower, such as cars accelerating and aeroplanes flying past, and sounds which are associated with going up and down, such as going down a slide, going up in a lift or a hot-air balloon.

EXTENSION

Everyone has a small cut-out object – maybe an animal or something which is being learnt about at the time. As the teacher plays, each child in turn places their cut-out onto the wall or board in order – high or low or medium according to the note played. The end result will be a very simple graphic score which could be played back again.

PURPOSE
To develop children's ability to control their vocal pitch and become more aware of differences in pitch.

RESOURCES
Puppet, fluffy toy or rag doll.

REMEMBER
Do not do this activity all at once. Make sure that 1-3 is thoroughly covered before the inventive section 4-7 is tackled.

Where are you?

SONG

'Where are you?' sung to the tune of 'Tommy Thumb, Tommy Thumb where are you?' or make up your own tune.

(Leader:) 'Pooh bear, Pooh bear, Where are you?'
(Children:) 'Here I am, here I am. How do you do?'

1. Children in a circle. Select children to have a puppet (each will get a turn in time).

2. Sing the song together, changing the words 'Pooh bear' to suit the toy/puppet you are referring to. Encourage the child with the named toy to answer and then continue each in turn around the circle.

3. For children who are reluctant to respond, remind them that it's the puppet you want to respond. Help by singing the response with the child.

EXTENSION

All children stand in a circle with their hands behind their backs and their eyes closed. Hand out one puppet/toy secretly, so that only one child has been chosen.
Start with confident singers, and move on to reluctant singers. Being the important child may encourage reluctant singers to respond.

The child hides the puppet, maybe behind a screen. When they are ready to sing, they bring to the puppet from behind the screen to sing without showing themselves. Children can sing 'in the voice' of their puppet.

PURPOSE

To encourage solo singing.

RESOURCES

Five or six puppets/ fluffy toy characters possibly brought from home

REMEMBER

Allow for a variety of responses. Some children may sing the full response, others may answer in a spoken voice, some may just say, 'Here', while others may not say anything but may animate their puppet.

Hello Anjali!

SONG

'Hello Anjali' sung to the tune of 'Three Blind Mice'.
(NB – not too fast).

(All:)   'Hello Anjali'   Child: Hello friends
(All:)   'Hello Anjali'   Child: Hello friends
(All:)   'She's in the circle ready to play.'
         'She brought her singing voice with her today.'
         'Sing again for us if you may.'
         'Hello friends' (Anjali echoes – 'Hello friends').

1. Learn this first version of the song. Obviously you use the names of the children in your class. If the child (named Anjali in this example) is reluctant to reply (quite possible) sing with the child, or ask an assistant to sing with the child. Sometimes children will respond, but in a spoken rather than a singing voice.

2. Try a second version. Suggest to the child that she quietly finds a hiding place while the others close their eyes. They have to find her by her answer. When she responds, the children point to where they think the she is hiding.

(All:)   'Where is Anjali?'   (Child:) 'Over here'.
(All:)   'Where is Anjali?'   (Child:) 'Over here'.
(All:)   'She's in the room and ready to play'.
         'She's brought her singing voice with her today.'
         'Sing again for us if you may Child: 'Over here'.

3. The child who has found Anjali becomes the next one to sing the answer.

PURPOSE

To sing a solo passage in a song.

RESOURCES

A variety of pitched instruments including recorders.

A keyboard if available.

REMEMBER

This may encourage some reluctant singers, but often needs some confidence on the part of the child to respond.

What are you doing today?

SONG:

To the tune of 'Polly Put the Kettle On.'
(All)   'What has Jenny done today?
          What has Jenny done today?
          What has Jenny done today?'
(All/Solo)   'I/she played in the sand.'

(Solo)   'I have (she has) played in the sand,
          I have (she has) played in the sand,
          I have (she has) played in the sand,
          That's what I've done today.'

1. Sing the song until everyone knows it well.

2. Ask children to think of something they have done today, eg,
    played in the sand, splashed in puddles, bounced on the bed,
    jumped up and down. They might sing:

    'I played in the home corner',
    'I sat down and read a book'
    'I played outside in the sun.'
    'I made hand prints with red paint'.
    'I made patterns with the shapes.'

3. Sing the first verse together with all the children.

4. Either the whole class sings the second verse or if the child is
    confident they can sing it back by themselves. The child may
    need help with words to ensure it scans with the melody. This
    might be done before the start of the song.

5. Now sing the question to another child to answer.

PURPOSE
To sing solo passages
in a song.

REMEMBER

If a child is reluctant it
is all right to sing for,
or with them.

This is ideal for singing
at the end of the day
before home time,
to settle the children
and review the day's
events.

Echoes

1. Learn the well-known song, 'I hear thunder', sung to the tune of 'Frère Jacques'. You can find melody lines for songs at the Kickstart Music area of www.acblack.com/music.

2. This is a good example of an echo song. The leader sings each line, which is repeated (echoed) by the children.

CALL/LEADER	ECHO/CHILDREN
'I hear thunder'	'I hear thunder'
'Hark, don't you?'	'Hark, don't you?'
'Pitter patter raindrops'	'Pitter patter raindrops'
'I'm wet through.'	'I'm wet through.'

3. Encourage the children to respond on their own, but you/ other adult may sing quietly with them if they are reluctant.

4. Once the song is established, the children could add sound effects at the end of each line, for instance:

   'I hear thunder' – drums, tambours played quite loudly
   'Hark don't you?' – drums, tambours played quite softly
   'Pitter patter raindrops' – lots of chime and bell sounds such as chime bars, triangles, bells and notes on tuned percussion.
   'I'm wet through' – lots of shaking instruments, such as jingle bells, maracas, castanets and tambourines.

5. Try dividing the class – one group providing the sound effects as the others sing.

EXTENSION

Make up your own echo verses with vocal noises. What else makes a noise? Here are some ideas to start with:

'I hear buses' – (engine sounds)– ''vroom vroom clitter clatter'.
'I hear babies' – (babbling sounds) – 'gurgle gurgle coo coo'.
'I hear cows' – 'moo moo moo.'

PURPOSE
To join in responses in echo songs.

Train's at the station

SONG

Train's at the station. See a suggested tune at the bottom of the page or create an original melody.

Train's at the Station, but the train can't leave,
Cos we're waiting for (David) will he get on please?
Now there's (one) on board, hear the whistle blow,
And when we're all on board we'll be ready to go.
(*blow the whistle)

1. Children stand in a circle.

2. An adult is the engine driver and puts on a hat or other distinguishing mark. The adult walks round the circle, pausing by and naming a child who joins the train, (eg, David). The child could hold the teachers waist – or they could be joined with a ribbon.

3. Everyone sings the song inserting the name David – in line two, and the number 'one' in line three.

4. The whistle blows and the train sets off round the circle, and a second child is chosen to join the train. Their name is used in line two – and now there are two on board in line three...and so on.

5. As each child joins, the number goes up, until a chosen number is reached. Then the song starts over again.

EXTENSION

1. Try the same activity with a child as the engine driver.

2. Older children might sing numbers in another language, or EAL children demonstrate the numbers in their first language.

PURPOSE
To encourage participation in a cumulative number song.

RESOURCES
Hat which will serve as the engine driver's hat.

A whistle.

All melody lines can be found on p64 and the Kickstart Music area of www.acblack.com/music.

REMEMBER
This song would be a good welcoming song, or a song for the end of a session or the end of the day.

It is useful for developing counting skills from one upwards, as many counting songs count backwards.

Train's at the station but the train can't leave cos we're waiting for (Dave) will he get on please Now there's

(One) on board hear the whistle blow and when we're all on board we'll be ready to go

Exploring

This section includes activities which provide opportunities for children to explore and find a range of sounds: body sounds, sounds from the environment, from instruments and from soundmakers. They will categorise them, use them in various ways, order their sounds in patterns and begin to build a library of sounds to use in their later music making.

The animal ball

SONG

'The animal ball' to the tune of 'Baa baa black sheep'

'Here come the animals in a parade
First/next comes (name of animal) don't be afraid
Hear the (name of the animal) make their call
On their way to the animal ball.'

1. Organise the children into pairs, each representing pairs of animals. If they have masks to wear – even better.

2. The children parade in a line. This could be around the circle, or between two facing lines of children. At the start of each verse, another pair are chosen to make their sounds during the verse, or at the end of each verse. They also make the actions of the animals as they approach the animal ball, eg, leaping frogs, waddling penguins, prowling lions and sliding snakes.

3. Alternatively, as each pair of animals arrives at the ball, they continue to make their sounds so that there is a gradual build up of animal sounds.

PURPOSE
To explore vocal sounds

RESOURCES

Animal masks (optional).

Large floor space, with designated area for the animal ball.

We're very noisy

Try one or more of these actions with the children to find lots of sounds from their bodies. Do this activity many times over the year. The teacher makes the sounds and the children copy. When they have the idea, make up patterns with the sounds by repeating them a lot of times.

Hands

1. Clap your hands loudly, then softly, then loudly, then softly, until it can be controlled well.

2. Rub your palms together quickly, then slowly, then quickly, then slowly, until it can be controlled well.

3. Rub your sleeves, your knees, the table, lots of times and in rhythm. Make up a pattern with the sounds.

4. Tap/drum your fingers on anything in the room – the table, the wall, a book, tins, plastic.

5. Using one of the sounds above, one person starts and then eveyone joins in, one by one. Listen to the way the sound gets louder as each person joins in. After a while start to get softer. Do this by each child dropping out one by one.

Feet

6. Stamp your feet slowly – run on the spot – stamp slowly.

7. Slide your feet across the floor in socks or barefoot, listening to the sound as you go. Now just one person slides and everyone listens – is it louder or softer than before?

8. Tap very quietly with your toe. Can the children copy the quietness as well as the tapping? How many more sounds can the children think of?

PURPOSE
To explore body sounds by making sounds with our hands and feet.

REMEMBER

All these sounds can be used later when the children are adding sounds to stories.

Don't just use a sound once. Use it a lot of times and you will find you have a musical pattern.

Junk band music

1. Show the children a range of possible sound makers you have accumulated. Start with, for instance, paper and foil. 'Play' them to the children by scrunching, waving, scratching, rubbing, blowing them.

   Find a noise you all like and play it lots of times, for instance, scrunch, scrunch, scrunch, scrunch, scruncn, scrunch. Perhaps sing a little song and use the scrunch as an 'accompaniment' to it.

2. Ask for suggestions for ways to play some of the other sound makers you have collected.

3. Ask the children to talk about and describe some of the sounds in simple terms:

   Which is their favourite?
   - Is it loud or quiet?
   - Does the sound remind them of anything?
     (They may say the wind, a kettle, a hammer....)
   - Does the sound last a long time?
   - Is it a rough sound or a smooth sound?

4. Make a temporary wall display of some of the items, for example: corrugated card to scrape, tissue paper to scrunch, rubber bands to twang, foil to flap.

5. You can use any of the sounds you have found to accompany songs the children know.

EXTENSION

Make a sound with the sound maker then pass it round the group for children to make a different sound using the same item. For instance, paper might be flapped, rubbed, scrunched, stroked, tapped, flicked, waved and tugged.

PURPOSE
To explore and talk about sounds.

RESOURCES

A variety of sound makers such as paper, foil, wooden spatulas, plastic plumbing/rain pipes, bubble wrap, corrugated card, tins/ plastic bottles crisp tubes or other containers filled with dried pulses or lentils, kazoos, tissue boxes with rubber bands, cloth materials, soft toys.

REMEMBER

This activity is best done with a small group of children, perhaps in the music area.

All together now

1. Every child has an instrument or a sound maker.

2. The children watch the puppet closely. When it 'dances' the children play their instruments. When it is still they all stop playing and are as quiet as possible.

3. Once the children can follow the puppet closely, they find a tapping sound on their instrument for when the puppet dances.

4. Ask one or two of the children to show the others their tapping sounds. Does the sound remind them of anything (dripping tap, someone knocking on the door, hammering)?

5. Repeat this activity with the puppet, asking for shaking sounds. Then repeat again asking for scraping or rubbing sounds. Some instruments may remain silent when shaken, others may need a lot of thought to find scraping/rubbing sounds.

6. Again, ask other children to share their sounds, maybe with the puppet telling them when to play.

7. Talk to the children about which instruments can produce lots of sounds in different ways and which only have a few.

EXTENSION

Ask children to pass their instrument on to the next child in the circle occasionally so that they get to play on a variety of instruments.

PURPOSE

To find a variety of sounds on percussion, and different ways of playing them.

RESOURCES

Puppet, and a variety of percussion and sound makers – enough for one per child.

Shake shake

1. Find three distinctive sounds to play to the children, such as shaking maracas or a tambourine, tapping a drum or claves, a vibra-slap or guiro and xylophone.

2. Find actions to go with the sounds, for example:
   * Shaking maracas – shake hands in the air.
   * Tapping a drum – step around the room or clap hands.
   * Vibra-slap – jiggle and shake.
   * Chime bars – swirling and dipping.

3. Play the sounds in different sequences - the children make the appropriate actions to go with the sounds.

4. One child could make a new, different action, while a group of children respond with the appropriate sounds.

5. The children use paints or crayons, and draw or paint the feeling of their actions, for example, swirling, jiggling, shaking. They share their pictures for other children to interpret in sound

EXTENSION

Spend some time talking about the materials the instruments are made of and why they sound like they do:
* What's inside the maracas and why does it make the noise it does?
* What do our yoghurt pots/crisp tubes sound like?
* What have they got inside?
* The chime bar is made of metal and it rings.

PURPOSE
To identify and distinguish between different sounds.

RESOURCES
Various percussion instruments.

Drawing or painting materials.

The gentle drum

1. Place the four hoops on the floor and put an assortment of up to six percussion instruments and sound makers in the middle of a circle of children.

2. Ask a child if they can find a sound on one of the instruments that is loud. (This will depend in some cases how the instrument is played). Begin creating a group of loud instruments in one of the hoops (if you are using them).

3. Now ask another child to find a sound that is quiet, and start a different group of instruments (in a different hoop).

4. After sorting the instruments, ask the children if any of the loud instruments can play quiet sounds and vice versa. Help the children to understand that instruments can be played loudly and quietly.

5. Try also with more instruments and other words such as; hard, soft, smooth, wooden, short, long, happy; until there are four or more hoops.

6. Divide the children equally around the groups of instruments (hoops). One child is chosen as conductor. He/she points to groups in turn – the children playing their sounds according to the way they have been sorted (loud, quiet, hard, soft, etc).

PURPOSE
To understand that instruments can play a variety of sounds, and develop a technical vocabulary.

RESOURCES

A variety of instruments.

Sorting hoops (optional).

REMEMBER

Most instruments can be played either loudly or softly, and usually graded between the two. Try and work towards an understanding in the children that they are the ones who control the dynamics in how they play, how they use the beater or shake the instrument.

Which sound?

SONG

Sung to the tune of 'Hickory Dickory Dock'.

'Tap it or scrape it or shake
Which instrument here will you take?
To play along, at the end of our song
(pause and choose a child)
What are the sounds you will make?'

1. Place a selection of instruments in the middle of a circle of children. Teach the children a signal for stop, such as a hand raised.

2. Sing the song all together – a selected child chooses an instrument (in line three) and returns to their place while the song is sung.

3. The child demonstrates their sound briefly, then continues to play along while the others repeat the song, and a new child is selected to choose an instrument. Encourage all the other children to join in the song.

EXTENSION

As an alternative way of choosing the next child to play, make a bridge with two children joining hands. The rest of the children walk under the bridge, singing the song, 'London Bridge is falling down'. The child caught in the arms of the 'bridge' at the end, is in this way, chosen to be the next to play.

PURPOSE
To begin to play along in time with a song.

RESOURCES

A selection of instruments and sound makers.

REMEMBER

Don't expect children to be able to play in time to the songs if they are improvising a beat. They will get better at it if you do this activity many times over the year. However, having an adult playing as a role model can be helpful.

That's the way to do it!

1. Decide on some start and stop signals for the children to follow, for example, opening and closing your hand like a beak – or by following the actions of a puppet or a soft toy (ie, play when the puppet dances and stop when it is still).

2. The puppet can watch and tell the teacher who is especially good at stopping quickly.

3. The children play their instruments to the signals, finding different ways to play their instruments each time there is a new start signal.

4. If the children find it difficult to think of new ways, remind them that they can tap, shake or scrape their instruments in many different ways – or they can blow, sing or tap something as well.

5. Ask a child to share their way of playing with the others. Those with similar instruments could copy.

6. Ask the children if the sounds remind them of anything, eg, shakers – pebbles rolling on the beach, tappers, someone knocking on the door.

7. Repeat, choosing different children to demonstrate their sounds.

PURPOSE
To explore ways of playing percussion.

RESOURCES

A variety of instruments. Sorting hoops (optional).

Puppet, sock puppet, paper bag with sticky dot eyes, paper plate with drawn-on face.

Fill the break

SONG

Sung to the tune 'There was a princess long ago'.

'In the break I'll play my sounds,
Play my sounds, play my sounds.
In the break I'll play my sounds,
Play for you.'

1. Children learn the song.

2. The children tap along to the beat of the song on percussion instruments while the song is sung. To gauge the beat of a song try walking in time to the song as well.

3. Choose a child to improvise playing their instrument while the others sing the song. The improvisation might take a number of different forms. For instance the child might:
   - Play simple sounds.
   - Tap the beat.
   - Create a simple rhythm.

4. Now repeat the activity, pausing between each rendition of the song whilst a child improvises a fill – for instance,
   Tap, 2, 3, 4, or rattle tap tap rattle.

PURPOSE

To encourage children to develop simple improvisation skills.

REMEMBER

Help the children to learn to play carefully and quietly. Give out some tuned percussion instruments as well as untuned ones. It will sound more interesting. If xylophones are used – encourage children to play with both hands.

GLOSSARY

Tuned instruments – instruments with notes which can make a tune, with notes of varied pitches, eg, chime bars, a piano, a recorder and a xylophone.

Untuned instruments – instruments which have the same pitch all the time and cannot play a tune. They are mostly used for rhythm, such as drums, tambourine, a triangle.

I hear one sound

SONG

'I hear one sound' to the tune of 'Frère Jacques'.

'I hear one sound, I hear one sound,
So can you, so can you.
Add another sound please, add another sound please,
Now there's two, now there's two'.

'I hear two sounds, I hear two sounds,
So can we, so can we.
Add another sound please, add another sound please.
Now there's three, now there's three'.

I hear three sounds, I hear three sounds,
Let's have more, let's have more.
Add another sound please, add another sound please,
Now there's four, now there's four.

1. Learn the song until everyone knows it well.

2. Decide on a number to count up to, say five, and give five children an instrument each. Then number the children one to five.

3. Children will take it in turns to accompany the song with a sound of their choice. Child number one plays their instrument during the singing of the first verse 'I hear one sound'. Other players keep their instruments quiet until their number verse is sung. Try and help the children to play in time to the song.

4. Try other songs which have simple counting rules, eg, 'Five currant buns', 'Ten green bottles'. As each object disappears, make sounds on instruments, eg 'and if one green bottle, should accidentally fall (crash on a cymbal),…there'd be nine green bottles…'

PURPOSE
To find appropriate sounds to accompany songs and play with control.

Creating

This section includes activities which will encourage children to discover sound, ways to combine those sounds to make simple musical patterns and sequences. They will be given opportunities to invent their own music and perform it to others.

Simple symbols

1. Play a sound on an instrument/sound maker (eg, tap a drum or a cymbal, shake maracas, rub a tambour skin, run a stick along the radiator).

2. Ask the children to draw the sound. The children may respond in a variety of ways. Some may draw the instrument, some may make dots and squiggles, others may draw shapes or write numbers.

3. Almost anything is acceptable as long as the children find a way of recording the sound on paper and that it means something to them. By doing this, they are producing a musical symbol.

4. Sort children into pairs with an instrument. Ask them to find a sound they like on their instrument – and again, find a way of representing the sound visually. Repeat this activity but with a second instrument.

5. Each pair of children decides which sound to play first and second. They put their drawings in the order they want and play them from the drawings/symbols (just like following musical notes or a musical score).

6. Children go on to work in groups of three or four, again deciding on an order for their symbols and sounds.

7. Stick their drawings/symbols onto backing paper for display and perform from them.

PURPOSE
To listen carefully and find simple ways of recording sounds on paper.

RESOURCES
Blank scrap paper and crayons

Tuneful stories

1. Demonstrate moving up and down in pitch with an up-ended xylophone (see similar instructions in 'Up and down', pg 38).

2. Tell some well-known stories. The children, or you, insert appropriate pitch notes to go with characters – for example:

   Goldilocks
   High notes for - Baby bear's bowl/chair/bed.
   Middle notes for - Mummy bear's bowl/chair/bed.
   Low notes for - Daddy bear's bowl/chair/bed.
   Stepping up the xylophone when she walks upstairs.

   Jack and the beanstalk
   Glissandos (sliding up/down notes with a beater) - the beanstalk growing and the giant falling.
   Stepping up/down the xylophone - Jack climbing/coming down the beanstalk.

   Jack and Jill
   Tell the story (perhaps before recalling the song).
   Glissandos down - falling down the hill.

3. Retell the stories, finding sounds for other aspects:
   Goldilocks
   Paper sounds - the leaves/ breeze in the trees.
   Wooden sounds - the bowls and the chairs.
   Repeated simple melody - running away through the woods.

   Jack and the beanstalk
   Shakers - the bag of beans.
   Cymbal taps - the golden goose.
   Low drums - the giant's footsteps.

   Jack and Jill
   Sing the song – pausing for the sound effects.
   Scraping guiros - winding up the pale of water.

PURPOSE
To encourage children to incorporate pitch in their musical stories

RESOURCES

A selection of tuned percussion

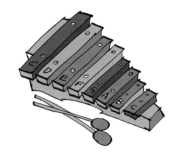

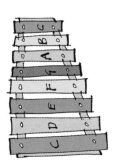

Picture sequences

1. Share instruments amongst the children. For example, if you have a photo of a guiro – then three or four children have a guiro if possible. If you have limited resources, use homemade sound makers which produce a similar sound. Make sure all children have an instrument or sound maker that corresponds with a photo.

2. Hold up photos in turn. The children playing their instruments when the photo of their instrument is held up. (This helps direct children's attention to the photo – a precursor to score/ music reading).

3. Agree on a simple sequence for the photos. Depending on the experience of the children, this may be a short sequence or a sequence with repeat photos.

4. Spend some time finding different sequences. Can the same instrument(s) play more than once in a sequence?

5. Children work in small groups with a helper, with photo sets and percussion, to develop a sequence and the skill to perform the sequence accurately. While children are working, pause everyone occasionally to listen to how a group is progressing.

6. Performance time. Children prepare their group to perform to the rest of the class. Alternatively, make each group sequence part of a longer class sequence.

7. Groups can be named 'A', 'B', 'C' etc. – and an even longer sequence can be developed by making a sequence of the letters eg, A–B–A–C–A–D–A.

8. Children might make a display of their final sequences in photos or drawings, put together as a large class score.

PURPOSE
To develop sequences and patterns in music.

RESOURCES

Sets of photos, produced from your classroom instruments. Alternatively search for images online or photocopy and use the ones in this book

Sound builder

1. Each child has an instrument or sound maker (which could be a vocal sound).

2. Introduce clear signals to stop and start playing (eg, pointing for start/hands up for stop). Practise this before you do anything else.

3. Everyone has a minute to find what their instrument or voice can do and make a short pattern they want to play. Give the 'stop' hand sign.

4. Point to one individual child to play.

5. Point to a second child who joins the music, and so on.

6. Build the sound – then use a stop sign (hand raised) to stop some of the sounds.

7. Now encourage a child to become the 'Sound builder'.

8. The child explores different combinations of instruments and voices playing together, by starting and stopping different children at different times. Try and listen to the result. You will hear layers of different sounds from different parts of the room.

EXTENSION

Group children together in categories of sound - such as all wood, all metal, all tapping sounds, all vocal sounds, all shaking sounds. The conductor moves from one group to another. Talk about the results with the children.

PURPOSE
To explore different combinations of sound, and follow start/stop signals.

RESOURCES

A variety of percussion and sound makers, and voices.

Animal crackers

1. Discuss the pictures with the children and what sounds they might use to represent them. Try making body sounds and 'sounds around' (see 'Junk Band Music' p47 for examples) to start with and add other sounds when you see that they are getting the idea.

2. Do each picture in turn. For example, they might make their musical pictures like this:
   - **Elephant** – slow plodding sounds with foot stamping and a drum, plus vocal trumpeting sound.
   - **Mouse** – fast scraping and tapping sounds with the fingernails on a table, and vocal squeaking.
   - **Butterfly** – fast, high sounds on chime bars and fluttery noises with the voice.

3. Group the children to play each picture. Then move from one picture to another while they play their music to it. Allow them time to modify it if it's obvious that it would improve.

EXTENSION

1. The children find simple melodies on xylophone or glockenspiel for the animals in the pictures – slow and low, fast and high.

2. Try adding sounds to songs with animals such as 'Old Macdonald' or 'Hickory Dickory Dock'.

PURPOSE
Explore vocal sounds, instrumental sounds and sounds around.

RESOURCES
Pictures of four or five animals, for example, cat, butterfly, horse, elephant, lion.

Signature tunes

1. Place three or four chime bars in the music area, with a pair of beaters.

2. Invite children to work on their own in the music area – to make up a very short melody that they can remember and repeat without mistakes, for example:

    > C – D – C – D – E
    > C – D – C – D – E
    > C – D – C – D – E

3. The children develop their own personal melodies. Give them plenty of time to practise and extend them. They might prefer to sing something but make sure they repeat the same thing every time.

EXTENSION

1. In a small group – listen to each child's personal 'signature tune'.

    It is possible some tunes will be exactly the same. Don't worry about this. Ask each child to play their tune in turn. Now use the children's names to decide on an order to play all the tunes one after the other, to make up a longer piece.

    The children play their tunes in turn, attempting to follow on from the last tune without too long a gap. If you feel they can handle it, ask them to play their tunes to the rest of the class.

2. When the class has heard most of the tunes, see if they can remember whose they were.

    Some of the children hide behind a screen. Ask the other children to listen to each of their signature tunes. One child plays their tune. Can the rest of the class identify which child played their signature tune?

PURPOSE
To create simple melodies

RESOURCES
Assorted chime bars

Three billy goats gruff

Choose a well-known story with strong characters and/or events which suggest the use of sound. Stories with animals and a strong sense of place, objects, or onomatopoeic words all provide good opportunities for sound. Here we use the traditional story, 'Three billy goats gruff'. It has a good sense of place (a stream rippling under a rickety bridge), strong characters (three different sized goats and a troll) and onomatopoeic words such as 'trip trap', or 'trippety trot' for the goats' hooves.

1. Read or tell the story to the children, with pictures if possible.

2. Remind the children of the elements in the story and talk about and find appropriate sounds to accompany them. For example:
   • Goats in the meadow - vocal bleating, munching.
   • Birds and butterflies – fast, high glockenspiel/triangles.
   • Goats trotting - coconut shells/woodblock.
   • Stream - chime bars/xylophone/rainmakers.
   • The troll - vocal growling.
   • The large goat butting the troll - vocal 'weee'.
   • Splash of the water - loud drum and cymbal.

   Give the children time to try the sounds out and practise them to see if they are sure what to do.

3. Decide which children are to be responsible for specific sounds/narration. Get everything ready to start.

4. Read the story again, allowing time for the sounds to illustrate the story and supporting the children to play at the right times.

EXTENSION

1. Create a role play area with costumes or props for the children to act out the story on their own.

2. Make an audio recording of the story with the sound effects.

PURPOSE
To develop the ability to add vocal as well as percussion sounds to a story.

RESOURCES

Various instruments and sound makers available to choose from.

Familiarise yourself with the traditional story of the 'Three billy goats gruff'.

The illustration below is available online for you to print and enlarge. Visit the Kickstart Music area of www.acblack.com/music.

Trails

1. Talk about what you see when you go to the park – swings, dogs, children running about, leaves falling. Create a simple trail picture such as the example below.

2. The children try and find some vocal or body sounds to represent the characters or events. For example:
   • Leaves falling – fluttering fingers, rubbing sleeves, singing a falling tune.
   • Children running about – running and stamping sounds, singing 'runabout, runabout, runabout' fast.
   • Swings – vocal swishing sounds from side to side.

   They then explore percussion and other soundmakers for additional sounds:
   • Leaves falling – glockenspiel glissandi down.
   • Children running about – tambourine shaking.
   • Swings – rubbing the table or a drum skin from side to side.

3. Divide the children into groups. One group for each picture you have discussed. Give each group time to practise their section.

4. Performance time. Pin the picture up and point to each one in turn. Each group plays their picture music. You can revisit some of the pictures if the children want to play them again. You would revisit them in the park.

PURPOSE
To follow a simple score and start/stop in the appropriate place.

RESOURCES
Trail ideas such as the one below, based on children's recent experiences, or imagined events. For this activity we have visited the park.

REMEMBER
This is a complete performance and composition project. You can do it in little bits, in groups or as a whole class, in one session, or over several weeks. You can visit other places and do the same exercise again but with quite different musical results.

Sounds of the seaside

1. Talk about seaside holidays and what you might expect if you went on one. Use a big picture of the seaside or video to help children who have never been, or adapt the idea for a real outdoor experience you have had together.

2. Sing a new version of 'Old MacDonald' and explore vocal sounds to go with the song. For example:

   'By the sea the other day, E-i-e-i-o
   We discovered crashing waves, E-i-e-i-o
   With a (wave sounds) here, and a (wave sounds) there'.

   Or 'discover' any of the following and make their sounds - calling gulls, cooling sand, an old lighthouse, lots of pebbles, chalky cliffs, sailing boats, secret pools, scary caves, donkey rides, an ice-cream stall, sticky rock.

3. Use sound cards and explore sounds to go with them. Give a card each to small groups of children. They try to match the sounds marked on the cards. For example:
   • Waves: rising, falling, crashing and rolling
   • Sea gulls: soaring, gliding and swooping
   • Pebbles: rolling in a ball, scattering, being pulled this way and that.

4. Using the cards as a score, create simple sequences, such as:

   | WAVES | SEAGULLS | WAVES | PEBBLES | WAVES |

5. Point to the cards in sequence. The children make appropriate sounds as you point to their cards.

6. Divide the class. One group builds up the accompanying sounds as the other group performs the song.

7. Ask children to create their own sound card sequences for others to perform. They could glue their sequences on to backing paper to keep a record of their compositions.

PURPOSE
To structure sounds into simple patterns.

RESOURCES
Pictures of the seaside. Search for images and short video snatches on the Web.

Sound cards with seaside words on them.

Resources

EQUIPMENT

Many of the activities in the book can be done without any instruments or soundmakers, or with simple sound makers (such as home-made or found objects), but it is always desirable to build a collection of good quality and easily accessible instruments. **Pitched instruments** might include xylophones, glockenspiels, chime bars and ocarinas, as well as piano, keyboards and other instruments children are learning in school, such as steel pans, trumpets or violins. **Unpitched percussion instruments** might include various sized drums and tablas, cymbals, bells and other resonant instruments, tambourines, rattles and other shakers, guiros and other scrapers. **Good quality beaters** are very important in getting the best quality sound from these instruments.

SONGS AND ACTIVITIES

No list could ever be comprehensive in an area such as this. There are many more songbooks as well than those listed here and teachers will have a list of their own songs whilst being unaware of the origins. Some examples include 'Okki-Tokki-Unga', 'Three Singing Pigs', 'Three Rapping Pigs', 'Three tapping teddies', 'Sonsense Nongs', 'Bobby Shaftoe, Clap your Hands', 'Someone's Singing, Lord' and 'Tam Tam Tambalay'. For all melody lines, extra information on resources and a full song index visit the Kickstart Music area of www.acblack.com/music.

RECORDED MUSIC

Recent major advances in technology mean that every classroom with a computer and amplification (eg, via a whiteboard system) can now play (and record) music. With the ease of use of the internet CD's are looking dated. Compilation CDs offer a useful introduction to listening, and music educational shops and publications often provide music suitable for use in early years and primary schools. Substantial information and guidance is to be found at the Kickstart Music area of the website (www.acblack.com/music).

Use the internet to access:

- Music for listening, either online, to stream or as downloads.
- Video clips for composition, to watch or to download.
- Free software for composing and manipulating music.

Throughout the book are ideas for music to use with the activities. These suggestions are in no way exhaustive or prescriptive and there are more ideas on the website. It is merely a list of music used successfully by many teachers for activities like these. There has been no attempt to include suggestions for modern popular music in this list, not as a result of any value judgement, but because fashion and availability is continually changing:

FOR MORE INFORMATION ON RESOURCES AND A FULL SONG LIST VISIT The KICKSTART MUSIC AREA OF WWW.ACBLACK.COM/MUSIC